About This Report

About the Urban Land Institute

The Urban Land Institute is a global, member-driven organization comprising more than 42,000 real estate and urban development professionals dedicated to advancing the Institute's mission of providing leadership in the responsible use of land and in creating and sustaining thriving communities worldwide.

ULI's interdisciplinary membership represents all aspects of the industry, including developers, property owners, investors, architects, urban planners, public officials, real estate brokers, appraisers, attorneys, engineers, financiers, and academics. Established in 1936, the Institute has a presence in the Americas, Europe, and Asia Pacific regions, with members in 80 countries.

The extraordinary impact that ULI makes on land use decision making is based on its members sharing expertise on a variety of factors affecting the built environment, including urbanization, demographic and population changes, new economic drivers, technology advancements, and environmental concerns.

More information is available at uli.org. Follow ULI on Twitter, Facebook, LinkedIn, and Instagram.

About the Center for Sustainability and Economic Performance

The ULI Center for Sustainability and Economic Performance is dedicated to driving more sustainable, environmentally responsible, and profitable outcomes in real estate development and investment, and to helping ULI members create healthy, resilient, and resource-efficient communities around the world. The center advances knowledge and catalyzes adoption of transformative market practices and policies that lead to improved sustainability, health, resource efficiency, and resilience.

About the Building Healthy Places Initiative

Around the world, communities face pressing health challenges related to the built environment. Through the Building Healthy Places Initiative, launched in 2013, ULI is leveraging the power of ULI's global networks to shape projects and places in ways that improve the health of people and communities.

Learn more and connect with Building Healthy Places: www.uli.org/health.

Report Team

Primary Author

Matthew Norris
Senior Manager, Content
Urban Land Institute

Contributing Author

Daron "Farmer D" Joffe
Founder, Farmer D Consulting

ULI Project Staff

Rachel MacCleery
Senior Vice President, Content

Billy Grayson
Executive Director, Center for
    Sustainability and Economic
    Performance

Ed McMahon
Senior Resident Fellow, Charles
    E. Fraser Chair for
    Sustainable Development and
    Environmental Policy

Reema Singh
Senior Associate, Content

Joanna Kramer
Intern, Content

James A. Mulligan
Senior Editor

**Laura Glassman, Publications
    Professionals LLC**
Manuscript Editor

Brandon Weil
Art Director

Anne Morgan
Lead Graphic Designer

**Mark Patrizio, Mark Patrizio
    Studio**
Illustrator

Craig Chapman
Senior Director, Publishing
    Operations

ULI Senior Executives

Ed Walter
Global Chief Executive Officer

Michael Terseck
Chief Financial Officer/Chief
    Administrative Officer

Cheryl Cummins
Global Governance Officer

Lisette van Doorn
Chief Executive Officer,
    ULI Europe

John Fitzgerald
Chief Executive Officer,
    ULI Asia Pacific

Adam Smolyar
Chief Marketing and
    Membership Officer

Steve Ridd
Executive Vice President,
    Global Business Operations

Contents

ULI is grateful to the Leichtag Foundation and the Colorado Health Foundation
for their support of this research.

THE GROWING TREND OF AGRIHOODS

Inspired by a growing understanding that development centered on food-production spaces can produce multiple benefits for individuals and communities while enhancing real estate performance, this report identifies best practices to aid developers and partner organizations in planning, creating, and operating projects with food-production areas.

The report responds to interest from ULI members and others who are seeking guidance and information about how to build agrihoods. Although many projects have been built in recent years, the field is relatively new, and until now few resources have been available for developers and others who would like to include production gardens and working farms as a central focus of their projects.

This research builds on the ULI report *Cultivating Development: Trends and Opportunities at the Intersection of Food and Real Estate.* It includes lessons learned from interviews with 24 ULI members and other agrihood practitioners, conducted from summer 2017 through spring 2018.

The report synthesizes information and insights from an agrihood-focused ULI retreat held in 2018 at Coastal Roots Farm/Leichtag Commons, a nonprofit community farm and education center in Encinitas, California. Leading experts from across the United States who are intimately involved in agrihood planning, development, and operations—including developers, planners, landscape architects, farmers, and nonprofit organization representatives—attended the retreat.

The report's authors hope that the best practices identified in this report will be helpful to those who are interested in building and developing agrihood projects and that they will inform the development of new projects that maximize their health, sustainability, social equity, and economic potential.

Prairie Crossing is a conservation community in Grayslake, Illinois, that provides homeowners with access to locally produced food from an on-site 100-acre (40.5 ha) farm.

ULI defines *agrihoods* as single-family, multifamily, or mixed-use communities built with a working farm or community garden as a focus.

Benefits of Agrihood Development

Agrihoods offer proven financial, health, and environmental benefits—to the stakeholders involved in their implementation, to surrounding communities, and to the planet.

■ *Agrihoods present a competitive edge.*
Of U.S. residents, 73 percent consider access to fresh, healthy foods to be a top or high priority when deciding where to live.[1] Interviews with agrihood project leaders show that including food-production spaces in residential or mixed-use developments can be less expensive to build and operate than certain other amenities, such as golf courses.

■ *Agrihoods promote health and social interaction.*
A community farm can be the centerpiece of a development, and associated programming and educational opportunities can foster community social ties. Studies show that people who have satisfying relationships are happier, have fewer health issues, and live longer.[2] Farms in communities provide residents with access to fresh produce, supporting positive health outcomes.

■ *Agrihoods can support an attractive return on investment.*
Many studies find as much as a 15 to 30 percent increase in the value of properties adjacent to parks and open space,[3] which can include working farms.

■ *Agrihoods can provide environmental benefits.*
Clustering development around working farms allows developers and communities to conserve productive farmland and natural areas and to mitigate increases in impervious surfaces.

■ *Agrihoods create jobs and support the local economy.*
Growing and selling food locally keeps food dollars in the community and provides jobs for farmers.

■ *Agrihoods are growing.*
The number of agrihoods in North America has been expanding in recent years. As of 2018, ULI has identified projects in 27 U.S. states and Canadian provinces.

TRENDS IN FOOD AND REAL ESTATE

ISSUES AND CONSIDERATIONS

PEOPLE

- Of adults, 39.8 percent—93.3 million people—are classified as obese in the United States.[4]

- Of U.S. residents, 16 percent—including 28 percent of African Americans and 25 percent of Latinos—say that healthy food is not available in their communities.[5]

- New and young farmers are interested in farming, but they often face barriers, including a lack of affordable farmland[6] and access to capital.

PLANET

- In the United States, 175 acres (71 ha) of farm and ranch land are lost each hour.[10]

- The average piece of produce is shipped 1,500 miles (2,400 km) before it reaches the plate.[11]

- More water is used worldwide to produce food that is thrown away than the total amount of water used by any single country.[12]

PROFIT

- Food has a unique ability to foster the creation of places in which people want to spend time; food-based businesses—including farms—can add value to real estate and support other components of development projects.[16]

- In 2013, 13 million U.S. residents between ages 18 and 34 grew food at home or in community gardens—an increase of 63 percent from 2008; food gardening–related spending by this group doubled during this period, reaching $1.2 billion in 2013.[17]

OPPORTUNITIES

- Urban agriculture has been shown to improve access to fresh produce, especially in low-income areas, and integration of public health programming can enhance knowledge and consumption of fruits and vegetables.[7]

- Community gardens have been shown to directly contribute to reductions in chronic disease and depression, especially when local residents are involved in gardening.[8]

- The number of food hubs—local centers that connect farmers to food-using businesses and support local food production and distribution—increased 770 percent between 2000 and 2016.[9]

- Eating seasonal foods that require less processing in combination with transporting products over shorter distances can lead to lower greenhouse gas emissions.[13]

- Local foods are often produced using organic methods, which can lower emissions associated with petroleum-based fertilizers.[14]

- Compact development and open-space preservation can help protect water quality by reducing the amount of paved surface and by allowing natural lands to filter rainwater and runoff before they reach drinking-water supplies.[15]

- Organic food sales in the United States totaled $47 billion in 2016—up 8.4 percent from the previous year—while sales in the overall food market increased by just 0.6 percent.[18]

- The number of farmers markets in the United States grew by 395 percent between 1994 and 2017.[19]

- Many studies find as much as a 15 to 30 percent increase in the value of properties adjacent to parks and open spaces, which can include working farms and community gardens.[20]

- Clustered development generally results in lower infrastructure capital expenditures and lower maintenance costs for local jurisdictions.[21] Agrihoods can include clustered development around preserved farmland.

AGRIHOOD FEATURES

KEY

1. Conservation area

2. Protected farmland

3. Food-production space

4. Farm service corridor

5. Event space

6. Clustered homes

7. Farm stand and market area

8. Grid pattern and connections to streets outside of development

9. Active transportation features

10. Trails

11. Edible landscaping

12. Clubhouse or community center

13. Shops and restaurants

14. Proximity to schools and other important community features

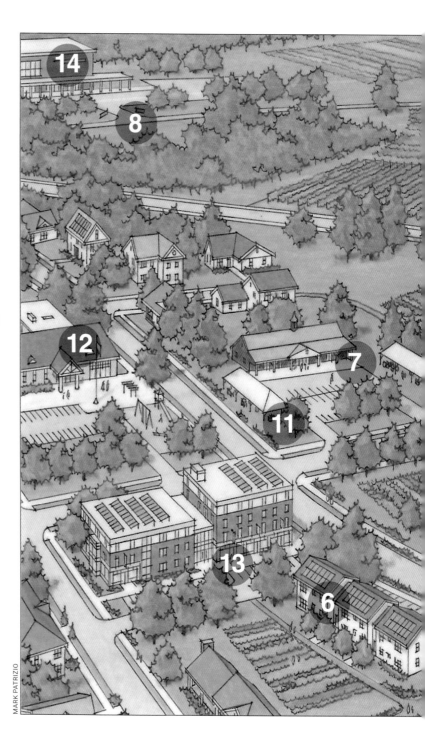

MARK PATRIZIO

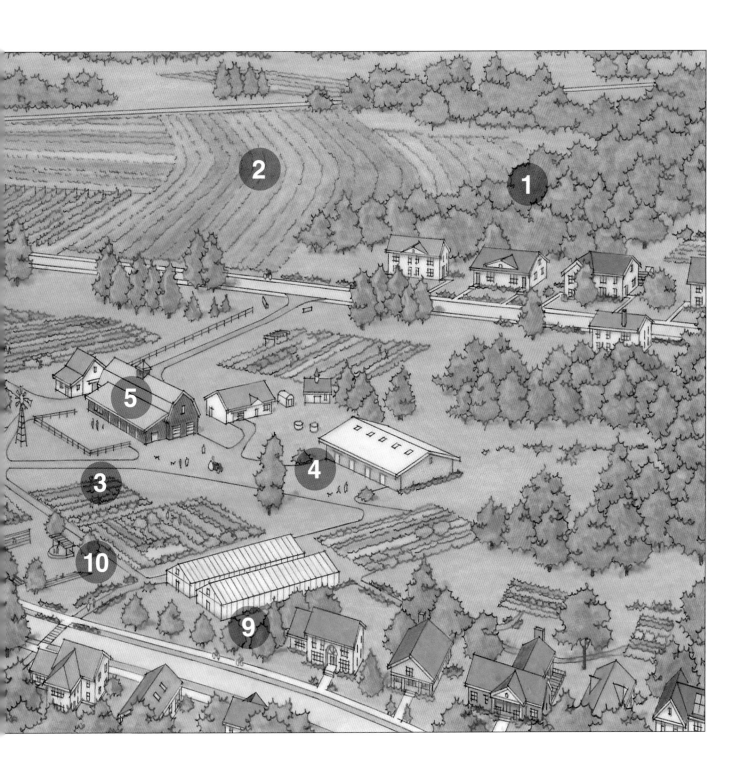

CHAPTER 2

BEST PRACTICES

PLANNING, DEVELOPMENT, AND OPERATIONS

People have long understood the fundamental role that food plays in health, well-being, and social interaction: most of life's great moments—holidays, weddings, birthdays, graduations—center around food.

The real estate industry plays a fundamental role in shaping how people access, purchase, and experience food. Agrihoods are part of a growing movement of food-centric development that is bringing consumers closer to the growers and producers of their food.

To build agrihoods, developers are forming innovative partnerships with landowners, farmers, nonprofit organizations, schools, public sector agencies, and other stakeholders, with positive implications for people and communities, as well as the bottom line for the development.

In many ways, planning, developing, and operating agrihoods is similar to planning, developing, and operating projects that are not built around food-production spaces. Agrihoods generally include a mix of homes, resident-focused amenities, and commercial spaces. Agrihoods are also underwritten by traditional lenders and rely on debt and equity financing—just like other projects.

By including a working farm as a central project feature, developers can unlock special advantages, ranging from reduced amenity costs, increased project marketability, and faster sales for residential properties, to opportunities for enhanced community social ties and access to land for current and would-be farmers.

Creating an agrihood is not necessarily more complicated than developing a project with more "traditional" amenities, but it does require a specific set of skills, innovative partnerships, and a significant commitment on the part of all project stakeholders.

Although agrihood development shares many similarities with the development of other projects, providing a farm as a project amenity may require real estate professionals to move outside their comfort zone and the standard development models. As key development amenities, farms require both upfront capital expenditures and ongoing operational support or subsidies—which can be offset by food sales, events, and other revenue streams.

By moving beyond the standard master-planned community development models and working with partners outside the "usual suspects," developers, owners, property managers, designers, investors, and others involved in real estate decision making can produce projects that benefit people, communities, and the planet while also generating profits.

The development of agrihoods is an emerging area of practice for the real estate industry. To help grow the field, ULI compiled emerging best practices for planning, developing, and operating agrihoods, organized under eight key topic areas. These best practices were identified through interviews with ULI members and other agrihood practitioners, as well as through insights from a 2018 retreat, research on projects from across the country, and other information collected by ULI.

By building agrihoods, real estate decision makers—including developers, investors, owners, and property managers—can leverage a focus on food production in development to create value, promote equitable economic development, enhance environmental sustainability, and improve public health.

ULI hopes the emerging best practices identified in this report will inform those interested in this approach to development and help grow the field of agrihood development, so that real estate leaders and other stakeholders can realize the potential benefits of agrihood development.

Ten Reasons Food Production Is a Growing Trend in Real Estate

1. People may not want to be personally engaged in agriculture every day, but they want high-quality food and agriculture to be part of their lives.

2. Consumers have an increased desire to be part of the "story of their food."

3. Residents often value farms and fresh food access over other development components.

4. Farms bring people together to share in food growing and related events.

5. Community farmers have a unique ability to inspire and educate area residents.

6. Farms can teach youth about food growing, nutrition, seasonality, and much more.

7. Health professionals increasingly promote the benefits of fresh, local produce to their patients.

8. Food-production spaces are less expensive to provide than certain other development amenities, such as golf courses.

9. Farms can serve as event spaces to offset the costs of food production.

10. Orienting development around farms can preserve the character of rural areas and make landscapes more productive and environmentally friendly.

(This list was identified by participants in ULI's Growing the Field retreat, March 21–23, 2018.)

Willowsford in Loudoun County, Virginia, is a 4,125-acre (1,669 ha) master-planned community that includes a range of single-family housing and a wealth of amenities, many related to fostering healthy lifestyles, including a working farm.

WILLOWSFORD

SUMMARY OF BEST PRACTICES

The development of agrihoods is an exciting area of innovation for the real estate industry. To help grow the field, ULI compiled emerging best practices for planning, developing, and operating agrihoods, organized under eight key topic areas.

Land

- Preserve natural lands and existing farmland by allocating space for agriculture, food production, and natural features in development.

- Create a land plan that optimizes farm productivity and opportunities for residents to engage with the farm.

Food

- Maximize food production and distribution methods.

- Align food production and distribution procedures with health, sustainability, social equity, and financial goals.

Finance

- Understand unique considerations related to agrihood financial models.

- Explore the agrihood "business case" at all stages of development.

Programming

- Position farms as community social hubs and settings for events.

- Engage residents and other stakeholders to ensure that on-site programs are inclusive and locally and culturally relevant.

Communications

- Focus on the farm in communications to generate broad community support and drive project success.

- Be intentional about crafting communications materials that include everyone and tell the "whole story."

....

Housing and Design

- Create housing and mixed-use development that leverage the advantages of farm-adjacent locations.

- Use innovative design and policy solutions to promote housing affordability and community social interaction.

....

People

- Understand the range of necessary skills for community farmers, and make decisions about hiring and management accordingly.

- Invest in homes for farmers and other farm employees.

....

Partnerships

- Collaborate with partners that share a common vision for agrihood development.

- Form partnerships to address health, sustainability, and social equity challenges through agrihood development and operations.

Land

Preserve natural lands and existing farmland by allocating space for agriculture, food production, and natural features in development.

› CONSIDERATIONS

» Many people like living near farms and protected green and open space, but "traditional" suburban development models do not protect or support these spaces.

» Infrastructure (roads, sewers, etc.) can be costly to provide if development follows suburban models with large lots and homes spaced far apart.

» Community reaction can be negative when development plans result in loss of farmland or green space, potentially resulting in costly project delays.

» Setting aside land for food production may require forgoing opportunities to build on "developable land."

› OPPORTUNITIES AND BEST PRACTICES

» Focus development around working farms and gardens, preserving existing farmland and conserving natural lands and features, such as streams and meadows.

» Create context-sensitive project density and development clusters.

» Take advantage of transfer of development rights and other public incentive programs, where available, to create project sites with appropriate allowable densities for agrihoods.

» Develop in or near areas with existing public infrastructure to minimize project costs, especially in communities that direct development by holding easements to permanently protect farmland.

"We created plans for 20 percent more residential units than would have been possible with traditional development practices and preserved over 70 percent of 'developable' land for agriculture and open space—all of this within 30 minutes of the world's busiest airport."

—STEVE NYGREN, PRESIDENT AND FOUNDER, SERENBE

Serenbe | Chattahoochee Hills, Georgia

Creating a connection with food, conserving land, and growing community: Serenbe is a 1,000-acre (400 ha) community that broke ground in 2004 in Chattahoochee Hills, Georgia. As of 2018, it includes 370 homes (single-family, multifamily, and live/work units), commercial and arts space, and four restaurants (a fifth was to open in fall 2018; a sixth will open in winter 2019), with eventual plans for a total of 1,200 homes and 3,500 residents. The development includes a number of food-based amenities, most notably a 25-acre (10 ha) professionally managed organic farm that forms the heart of the community. Serenbe also features an extensive nature trail system, conserves water through landscaping, and naturally treats wastewater for use in irrigation.

Serenbe has preserved a significant portion of some of the last open space near Atlanta, allowing for the creation of a community focused on food and interaction among neighbors.

KEY INSIGHT: CLUSTERING DEVELOPMENT

Agrihoods often cluster houses on a portion of developable land. By separating lot size from density, developers can provide the same number of units as a "conventional" development on less land. For example, instead of building 100 homes on one-acre (0.4 ha) lots, an agrihood might include 100 homes on quarter-acre (0.1 ha) lots with 75 acres (30 ha) of conserved open space and/or farmland.

Land

Create a land plan that optimizes farm productivity and opportunities for residents to engage with the farm.

〉 CONSIDERATIONS

» Required land uses for agrihoods differ significantly from traditional master-planned communities.

» Developers face financial and operational tradeoffs when determining appropriate agrihood farm size and location.

» Developers may lack in-house knowledge of where to place farms within project sites.

» Project stakeholders must balance needs when determining landownership structures and operational models for food-production areas.

〉 OPPORTUNITIES AND BEST PRACTICES

» Plan agricultural areas from a project's start to ensure they are in the appropriate places and well-integrated into the community.

» Partner with experts—including agricultural nonprofits and farm consulting businesses—to help determine optimal locations, layouts, circulation, and other key factors for setting up the farm for operational and programmatic success.

» Base farm size on clearly defined project goals:

- Create smaller farms if focus is on educational and experiential activities.
- Create larger farms to engage in more intensive agriculture.
- Consider startup and operating budgets to help determine farm scale and infrastructure.

» Set aside and provide appropriate space for farming operations (service corridors, tractors, large equipment, etc.) and establish clear boundaries for food-production areas.

» Determine appropriate farming infrastructure (irrigation, farming IT systems, electricity, lighting, ADA accessibility, security, etc.).

» Consider incentives for farmers to stay invested in projects, such as providing housing, affording land and/or business ownership opportunities, and offering administrative support.

Ownership and Governance Structures: Developer-Supported Farms

Typically, the developer is in control of the farm for several years while the project is being planned and built. During this period, the developer can help incubate the farm by managing initial financing/fundraising, hiring, marketing, and programming.

Before farm operations begin, the developer generally works with a management entity to create a transition plan to ensure that funding mechanisms and operational procedures are in place when the developer exits. This process allows the development team to guarantee the branding, marketing, programming, and financial health of the farm will be supported and aligned with the overall project goals.

Farms in agrihoods are often set up as nonprofits, because they provide several community benefits through education, food donations, and land preservation. These community farms are often not directly profitable because of their highly diversified crops and intensive community programming schedule. However, nonprofit farms can qualify for grants, corporate sponsorships, donations, and other forms of support. They are also able to develop a strong board of directors to help the farm grow and manage programs, partnerships, and staff.

Here are a few examples of how some agrihood farms are structured at different phases of a project:

- Developer owned and operated;

- Land trust ownership with nonprofit or for-profit farm management entity;

- Land trust ownership with lease or management agreement with farmer or farmers;

- Homeowners association–owned and operated by nonprofit or for-profit farm management entity;

- Public ownership and operated by nonprofit or for-profit farm management entity;

- Publicly owned and operated;

- Farmer-owned with operating agreement and ability to sell or transfer ownership or lease; and

- Nonprofit owned or leased with operating agreement and ability to sell or transfer ownership or lease.

KEY INSIGHT: FARM SIZE

■ Less than five acres (2 ha)

- Farms can work leanly and be highly engaging for residents and communities.
- Small farms require one to two full-time staff members (depending on production systems, the type of food produced, and amount of programming).
- They are typically more focused on education, experiences, and events with small-scale intensive production.

■ Between five and 20 acres (2 to 8.1 ha)

- Such farms run much like a four- to five-acre (1.6 ha to 2 ha) farm, with more room for production and programming space.
- They require ten to 20 full-time staff members.

■ Larger than 20 acres (8.1 ha)

- Farms of this size require more mechanization but can operate with fewer staff members because of greater efficiency from use of machinery.
- They require about ten full-time staff with potential for one to five additional staff members if the farm includes intensive on-site programming.

Food

Maximize food production and distribution methods.

› CONSIDERATIONS

» A lack of in-house farming knowledge in development companies can result in unrealistic expectations for farm productivity or types of food that can be produced.

» Education and communication between the farm and development teams are needed.

» Farms may not be financially self-sufficient, depending on size, project phase, overall goals, and whether revenue-generating events are allowed.

» Farms can take several years to reach full productivity, and fields may need to lie fallow during the off season in many regions of the United States.

› OPPORTUNITIES AND BEST PRACTICES

» Consult with farmers and other experts to determine what food to produce, at what scale, with what methods, and how food should be sold or distributed.

» Offset farm operational costs with food sales; farms may also need to rely on support from the development—especially during early project phases—in the form of free or subsidized land, contributions from transfer fees, homeowners association fees, and other mechanisms.

» Plan to devote land to farming for the long term; educate residents about farming practices to set realistic expectations for farm aesthetics and productivity.

» Appreciate and communicate food production challenges caused by seasonality and weather, pests and disease, and other challenges that farmers face.

» Consider food, worker, and visitor safety when designing facilities and setting up operating procedures.

"Farming is fundamentally different than the conventional landscaping that most developers are used to. Developers should partner with agricultural experts to manage farm assets and should consider hiring a facilitator to serve as the 'farm liaison' among all project partners."

—MARY KIMBALL, EXECUTIVE DIRECTOR, CENTER FOR LAND-BASED LEARNING

Types of Agrihood Food-Production Spaces

- Community farms

- Demonstration farms

- Small-scale/accessible-scale farms

- Edible landscaping

- Vineyards

- Orchards/olive groves

- Community gardens (professionally managed or community managed)

- Rooftop farms

- Farms or gardens at churches, schools, public land, corporate campus, senior centers, and retreat centers

- Controlled-environment agriculture, such as greenhouses, warehouses, and shipping containers and

- Land where homes cannot be built, such as utility easements

Prairie Crossing residents and the general public buy vegetables, fruits, eggs, and other farm products from different farm businesses at the Prairie Crossing Farm.

Grow Community, in Bainbridge Island, Washington, includes gardens that allow residents to cultivate food; surplus crops go to local food banks.

KEY INSIGHT: CONSIDERATIONS WHEN FARMING INCLUDES ANIMALS

- Potential benefits:
  - Positive marketing opportunities
  - Waste-recycling opportunities
  - Soil fertility benefits
  - Small-scale animals (i.e., poultry) are easier to manage
  - Grazing animals in larger projects can help with managing grasslands
  - Meat and dairy products can generate significant revenue

- Potential drawbacks:
  - Issues related to smell and noise
  - Issues with predatory species
  - Slaughtering of animals making people uncomfortable
  - Higher expenses related to infrastructure necessary for commercial meat and dairy production

Food

Align food production and distribution procedures with health, sustainability, social equity, and financial goals.

❯ CONSIDERATIONS

» Master-planned communities can lack spaces for food production and sales, which limits opportunities to tap into consumer demand for fresh, healthy, organic or local food.

» Residential and mixed-use developments can be isolated from surrounding areas, limiting opportunities to equitably address access to healthy food.

❯ OPPORTUNITIES AND BEST PRACTICES

» Sell and distribute food directly to residents and the surrounding community.

» Position farms as a community resource for healthy food access and related programming; consider "pay-what-you-can" farm stands.

» Consider organic and other certifications; leverage increased market interest in sustainably sourced products.[22]

» Grow culturally appropriate crops for customers and food donation partners.

Arbor House | Bronx, New York

Growing rooftop produce to promote healthy food access: Located in the Bronx, New York, Arbor House is a 120,000-square-foot (11,000 sq m) building with 124 units of affordable housing, developed by Blue Sea Development Company. Arbor House is located in an area with disproportionately high rates of chronic diseases, such as diabetes and heart disease. The development includes a number of features to promote healthy living, including a hydroponic rooftop farm. At 10,000 square feet (930 sq m), the farm allows residents to buy healthy produce grown on the farm, including vegetables and herbs; 40 percent of the produce will be available in the surrounding area through school, hospital, and food market programs. In addition to the healthy food grown on the roof, Arbor House includes features to promote physical activity, including indoor and outdoor fitness areas and prominently placed stairs.

Types of Agrihood Food Distribution Methods

Direct sales to consumers

- Farm stands—market price
- Farm stands—"pay what you can"
- Community-supported agriculture (CSA)
- Community "u-pick"
- Farmers markets

Wholesale

- Sales to restaurants and caterers
- Sales to distributors, aggregators, and food hubs
- Sales to institutions (schools, hospitals, seniors' centers, etc.)

Donations

- Local food pantries or food banks
- Gleaning/food recovery organizations
- Electronic benefit transfers (EBT) at farm stands and markets
- On-site donation pickups
- Off-site pop-up farm stands (donation or pay what you can)
- Donation of CSA shares
- Pick your own (free or subsidized cost)
- Food prescription programs in partnership with health insurance companies

Finance

Understand unique considerations related to agrihood financial models.

⟩ CONSIDERATIONS

» Agrihoods generate many qualitative benefits for a development that may not be quantifiable for a pro forma (including community engagement, brand equity, revenue generated from programming, and lower operating expenses than some other traditional amenities, such as golf courses); as a result, traditional financial analysis may undervalue agrihood benefits.

» Developers may not always be able to maximize land value with agriculture in all areas, especially in urban locations.

» Project operators cannot expect direct revenue from farming until several years after making an investment in a farm; therefore, developers with shorter hold cycles may see less of a financial incentive to create agrihoods.

» Agrihood development may require unconventional partnerships, agreements, and policy-related incentives, restrictions, and covenants.

⟩ OPPORTUNITIES AND BEST PRACTICES

» Understand that agrihoods are generally underwritten by traditional lenders and rely on debt and equity financing, like more traditional projects.

» Include lenders and potential equity partners in project visioning and planning from the start to gain buy-in and limit any hesitations related to investing in agriculture-centric projects.

» Move beyond usual sources of development financing to fund farm capital and operational expenditures.

» Seek local and national incentives—such as conservation easements, stormwater credits, state open-space tax credits, and funding from the U.S. Department of Agriculture and the National Resources Conservation Service Farm and Ranch Land Protection Program—to improve a project's financial position and cash flow.

» Link revenue models for the farm to the project's scale and mission; consider the financial impacts of selling

■ Produce;

■ Experiences;

■ Events, entertainment, and tourism opportunities; and

■ Views/proximity to open space.

Potential Sources of Funding for Farms Included in Development Projects

- ■ Development revenue
  - • Developer allowance
  - • Homeowners association fees
- ■ Production and services revenue
  - • Produce sales
    - — Direct—CSA, farm stand, farmers markets and/or online
    - — Wholesale—restaurants, caterers, grocers, aggregators, and/or institutions
  - • Value-added product sales (direct and/or wholesale)
  - • Pick your own (strawberries, pumpkins, blueberries, etc.)
  - • Plant sales
  - • Fees for garden and landscape services for residents
  - • Fees for composting service and finished product sales
  - • Community garden plot rentals

- ■ Program revenue
  - • Public programs (petting zoos, hay rides, corn mazes, farm-based discovery museum, etc.)
  - • Private programs (school field trips, summer camps, after-school programs, workshops, corporate retreats, etc.)
  - • Events (tours, weddings, birthdays, farm-to-table dinners, etc.)
  - • Wellness programs
  - • Venue rental
- ■ On-farm retail revenue
  - • Farm stands
  - • Nursery and/or garden centers
  - • Farm-to-table restaurants
  - • Culinary schools
  - • Breweries or wineries
- ■ Philanthropic revenue
  - • Grants (foundations, nonprofit, government, etc.)
  - • Individual donations
  - • Giving circles
  - • Fundraisers
  - • Sponsorships (cwworporate, naming, memorials, etc.)
  - • Social impact financing

"Developing an authentic agrihood requires an entrepreneurial spirit. This is a relatively new concept without many examples, which can create hesitancy if stakeholders, including lenders, aren't involved throughout the process."

—DWIGHT SAATHOFF, PRESIDENT, PROJECT FINANCE AND DEVELOPMENT, DEVELOPER OF THE GROW, ORLANDO, FLORIDA

Finance

Explore the agrihood "business case" at all stages of development.

〉 CONSIDERATIONS

» Depending on project context and local zoning, development around a working farm may lead to faster entitlements and permitting—because of greater public support—or may lead to delays in receiving entitlements and permits, especially in areas that do not allow clustered development or on-site event spaces as of right.

» Creating and operating farms differs from providing other traditional development amenities and requires a commitment on the part of all project stakeholders.

» Planning and operating agrihoods can be management intensive; developers must often make a significant time commitment when deciding to invest in these projects.

» Farms—especially those with community programming—require insurance coverage because farming can involve hazardous activities.

〉 OPPORTUNITIES AND BEST PRACTICES

» Accurately assess whether benefits outweigh associated costs when deciding to invest in agrihoods by exploring the full range of potential financial advantages that can accrue during all phases of development.

» Understand how farms can drive project value and generate positive returns on investment for developers, investors, and communities; use this information to make the case for investment to potential lenders and equity partners.

» Look to previous projects to better assess how an agrihood may be able to drive faster lease-up rates or higher rents and sales prices compared to traditional developments.

» Use other agrihoods and community-oriented farms as references for lenders, insurance brokers, bankers, city officials, and others who are not familiar with this concept.

» Assess and understand potential liabilities from food production and farm operations, including beekeeping, chickens and eggs, farm equipment, and develop a plan for addressing them.

The Business Case for Agrihoods

Planning and design	Project marketing	Project completion	Operations and maintenance
■ Stronger support for proposed developments through early community engagement related to farm preservation or creation	■ Ability to capture strong market demand for local food and experiences	■ Accelerated market absorption rates	■ Increased net operating income
■ Increased buy-in from influential stakeholders, including public officials and investors	■ Increased marketability from project differentiation	■ Potential for enhanced asset value through faster lease-ups and sales	■ Relatively low operational expenditures compared to some project amenities
■ Faster zoning approvals and entitlements in certain jurisdictions, thereby lowering project costs	■ Ability to create project branding based on farm	■ Ability to command sales or rental rates above comparable projects that lack farms	■ New revenue streams from food sales
■ Increased development density in localities that allow clustered development around farms or transfer of development rights	■ Increased project visibility due to media attention	■ Relatively low capital expenditure on farm compared to some other "traditional" amenities, such as golf courses	■ Potential revenue streams for providing public goods (i.e., green infrastructure)
■ Infrastructure efficiency through clustered development	■ Ability to use farm as event space in the early phases of a project to create buzz and attract buyers	■ Local, state, or federal incentives that reduce project cost through tax exemptions, reductions, and rebates	■ Revenue streams from on-site events
	■ Positive project exposure with target audiences from farm-branded products being used in restaurants and farmers markets		■ Long-term cost savings through resilience-promoting features
			■ Potential for better mortgage insurance rates from debt providers
			■ Potential for increased residential tenant retention
			■ Long-term real estate value appreciation from open-space adjacency
			■ Project resilience during economic downturns

Programming

Position farms as community social hubs and settings for events.

⟩ CONSIDERATIONS

» Programming is equally as essential to a project's success as design; developers cannot expect optimal benefits for projects and communities if farm areas lack activation and programming.

» Local zoning may limit or prohibit farm-oriented events or related facilities, limiting revenue generation potential.

⟩ OPPORTUNITIES AND BEST PRACTICES

» Provide educational opportunities in food production, gardening, nutrition to residents, schools, and other stakeholders.

» Facilitate resident interaction through farm-centered events to create a sense of place, ownership, affinity, safety, and security among neighbors and farm staff.

» Encourage residents to volunteer and participate in guided farm activities.

» Recognize the positive effect programming can have on a project's financial success; create a dedicated budget for events, and consider funding events and workshops through homeowners association dues.

» Work with community stakeholders and public officials to gain zoning approval for on-site, revenue-generating, farm-oriented events.

» Consider effects of having large events on the farm, including the physical wear and tear to the site and the farm's production.

» Partner with organizations and companies on programs and events to expand capacity without overburdening farm staff.

- -

"Homes at Prairie Crossing are selling at a 30 percent premium compared to comparable homes in neighboring communities. This is likely in part due to resident demand for living alongside the farm and conserved native landscape."

—BRAD LEIBOV, PRESIDENT AND CEO, LIBERTY PRAIRIE FOUNDATION

Examples of Programs Hosted at Community Farms

- Volunteer programs
- Farm and nature tours
- Classes and workshops related to farming, gardening, homesteading, backyard chickens, cooking, arts, edible landscaping, water conservation, etc.
- Internships, apprenticeships, and farm training programs
- Farm-to-table events connecting farmers, chefs, and community
- Corporate events
- Celebrations and fundraisers
- Faith-based programs

- Youth-related programs
  - School field trips
  - Camps
  - After-school programs
  - Preschool on the farm
  - Family programs
- Public programs
  - Farm festivals
  - Family programs
  - Petting zoo and other self-guided activities
  - Vendor fairs

Programming

Engage residents and other stakeholders to ensure that on-site programs are inclusive and locally and culturally relevant.

› CONSIDERATIONS

» Farms are natural settings for the type of community social interaction that residents increasingly demand, but those who do not live on site may not always feel welcome.

» Agrihood operators may miss opportunities to create locally and culturally relevant programming that can drive long-term project success if they do not empower area residents and stakeholders to participate in event planning.

› OPPORTUNITIES AND BEST PRACTICES

» Make inclusion, diversity, and community engagement beyond the development area central in event planning.

» Cultivate a healthier, more connected community by offering programs to bring diverse populations together.

» Set up channels for residents to communicate and plan events from the "bottom up."

» Implement thoughtful hiring practices for event planning and management; consider diversity and cultural representation.

» Host nutrition and healthy eating classes, and include residents from the surrounding area.

"People want to be part of a larger story. The production garden at Aria Denver grants residents access to fresh produce and facilitates social interaction through a variety of classes and community events. On top of that, it makes a positive difference in terms of the marketability of the project."

—SUSAN POWERS, PRESIDENT, URBAN VENTURES LLC

Aria Denver | Denver, Colorado

Growing and selling food on site to promote health, social intersection, and youth job training: Aria Denver is an infill community designed with a focus on the health of its residents and the surrounding neighborhood. Aria is being developed on a 17.5-acre (7.1 ha) site that was formerly home to the Marycrest Convent in North Denver. The development contains a 1.25-acre (0.5 ha) production garden, a greenhouse, and various other features to accommodate access to fresh produce.

Codevelopers Urban Ventures LLC and Perry Rose LLC have built 72 affordable rental apartments, 13 townhouses, and 28 for-sale cohousing units; 450 homes in total are planned. Other sites have been sold to outside developers, and 80 additional residential units and a commercial center are under construction.

The project includes a pay-as-you-can farm stand, pocket gardens, fitness equipment, and a wide assortment of classes for the community on various aspects of gardening, nutrition, and fitness. "Over the years that this development has taken place, we have seen increased interest from the residents and neighborhood in general in the activities associated with the urban farm," notes developer Susan Powers, president of Urban Ventures LLC. "Now, residents think of it as their own and have volunteered to raise funds to keep it viable and growing."

Aria Denver includes a mix of housing types, with a goal of encouraging social interaction and multigenerational living.

URBAN VENTURES

Communications

Focus on the farm in communications to generate broad community support and drive project success.

> CONSIDERATIONS

» Without a clearly defined project identity, crafting messages that resonate with prospective homebuyers and renters is difficult.

» Consumers increasingly demand local food, products, and experiences,[23] yet communications about new real estate developments often lack a focus on these areas.

> OPPORTUNITIES AND BEST PRACTICES

» Align the branding and narrative of the overall development with the farm to ensure a consistent and authentic message and brand.

» Leverage media interest in agrihoods and share how developer-supported agriculture can promote community social ties, access to local food, and preservation of farmland.

» Share testimonials from current residents and event participants about their experiences in engaging with the farm and farm-related activities.

» Create communications materials that explain the history and ecology of the land and the environmental and social impact of maintaining land for farming.

HILLWOOD COMMUNITIES

Focusing on food in agrihood communications can help convey project value to a wide range of groups, potential residents, and project partners.

Harvest | Northlake/Argyle, Texas

Making an organic farm the centerpiece of a new community: Located in Northlake/Argyle, Texas, Harvest is a 1,200-acre (486 ha) master-planned development consisting of 3,200 single-family homes and 120 acres (49 ha) of mixed use and high-density residential in planning. Developed by Hillwood Communities, Harvest home prices range from the high $200,000s to the mid $500,000s. Since the project opened in 2014, Harvest is more than 60 percent built out and is averaging 400 sales per year. The project revolves around the proud farming heritage of the original landowners. At the heart of the Harvest community is a working commercial CSA farm, operated by a professional farmer who shares his expertise with homeowners, "Harvest Littles," and their parents. Many Harvest neighbors enjoy the pride of growing their own vegetables and herbs in raised private plots available for lease for $90 yearly. The community has adopted the North Texas Food Bank as its charity of choice, having donated more the 23,000 meals since its first residents moved to Harvest in 2014.

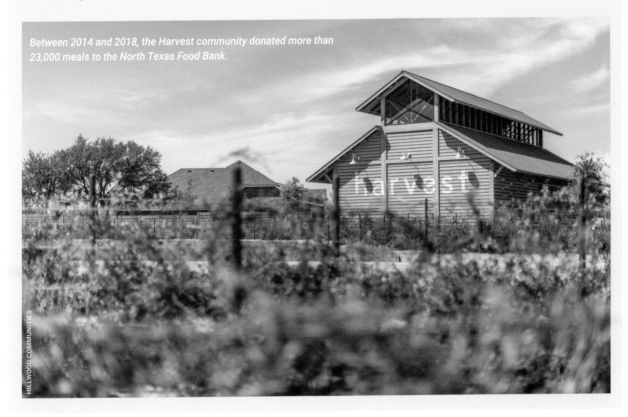

Between 2014 and 2018, the Harvest community donated more than 23,000 meals to the North Texas Food Bank.

HILLWOOD COMMUNITIES

"Our residents are our strongest brand ambassadors—especially given how little commercial and professional infrastructure had been in place in the surrounding area to draw people here."

—TOM WOLIVER, VICE PRESIDENT OF PLANNING AND DEVELOPMENT, HILLWOOD COMMUNITIES

Communications

Be intentional about crafting communications materials that include everyone and tell the "whole story."

› CONSIDERATIONS

» Key groups that could benefit from, and contribute to, the vitality of agrihood developments are sometimes excluded from targeted communications efforts.

» Agrihood developers may face difficulties in reconciling official communications about the benefits of "farm living" with the situation on the ground at a project's start (i.e., it may take several years for farms to become productive).

› OPPORTUNITIES AND BEST PRACTICES

» Employ a communications team that is culturally and ethnically diverse and that brings a range of professional experiences to go beyond the usual suspects in crafting project communications.

» Create communications materials that convey project value to a wide range of groups, potential residents, and project partners, including the following:

- The commercial, retail, and light industrial sectors;
- Those in the residential rental market;
- Schools and nonprofit groups;
- Busy people/those who work nontraditional hours; and
- Future farmers.

» Take the time to craft messages that tell the "whole story"; encourage resident buy-in by detailing how farms operate, the level of resident access to the farm, and when produce will be available.

» Consider starting the farm ahead of the rest of the development to create a sense of place and begin telling the story of the place through events and engaging the community.

KEY INSIGHT: RECENT MEDIA HEADLINES ON AGRIHOODS

"Are 'Agrihoods' the Cure for the Common Suburb?"

"Growing Agrihoods: The Next Frontier in Urban Revitalization"

"Seeds of a New Community: Farm Living Takes Root in the Suburbs"

"Millennials Are Ditching the Golf Communities of Their Parents for a New Kind of Neighborhood"

"Goodbye Golf Course, Hello Olive Grove!"

Agrihood communications can promote farm festivals, concerts, and other events.

Housing and Design

Create housing and mixed-use development that leverage the advantages of farm-adjacent locations.

› CONSIDERATIONS

» Developing housing and mixed-use buildings adjacent to food-production areas presents unique challenges related to the externalities of farm operations.

» Developers and project operators face tradeoffs when determining the appropriate balance of housing, mixed-use development, open/community spaces, and revenue-generating project amenities.

» Farmers often work very early in the morning and late into the evening and use loud equipment; farms can also attract pests and wildlife.

› OPPORTUNITIES AND BEST PRACTICES

» Include farmers in design decisions to ensure the farm has appropriate buffers between public and private areas to be both conducive for farming and for public engagement with the farm.

» Incorporate mixed-use development, including restaurants and retail, adjacent to food-production areas to create synergies with farms.

» Incorporate adjacent parks, trails, and natural areas to create synergies with the farm.

» Consider including revenue-generating project amenities to maximize project returns on investment and offset farm startup costs.

"Residents enjoy easy access to local food as well as the ability to volunteer close to home. The Esencia Farm location is along a street adjacent to homes, which makes it ideal for easy accessibility and site visibility."

—AMAYA GENARO, DIRECTOR, COMMUNITY SERVICES, RANCHO MISSION VIEJO

Rancho Mission Viejo | Orange County, California

Preserving land for food production in a vast mixed-use development: Rancho Mission Viejo is a planned community on 23,000 acres (9,300 ha) that includes organic fruit orchards, vegetable farming areas, and cattle ranching. Nearly 17,000 acres (6,900 ha) of "the Ranch" are being preserved as open space, while 6,000 acres (2,400 ha) are being developed into residential and mixed-use villages. Ultimately, Rancho Mission Viejo will provide 14,000 homes, of which 6,000 will be reserved for people 55 years of age and older within intergenerational villages. The project will also offer sites for schools, parks, clubhouses, and other recreational amenities, as well as employment and retail centers.

The first village on the Ranch is Sendero, which includes two communal farms and 941 homes that sold out by 2016. The second village is Esencia, which is for sale as of 2018 and includes a communal farm. Upon completion, Esencia is planned to include 2,485 homes for sale, including single-story homes for those 55 and older and 262 rental apartments. Currently, homes are priced from the high $400,000s to over $1 million. The Ranch is expected to encourage environmental sustainability by including communal farms that produce food for residents to buy and offering educational programs in farming, raising chickens, and sustainably grown food preparation.

Rancho Mission Viejo, in Orange County, California, sits on 23,000 acres (9,300 ha), of which 17,000 acres (6,900 ha) are being preserved as open space.

Clustering development around working farms allows developers and communities to conserve productive farmland and natural areas.

Housing and Design

Use innovative design and policy solutions to promote housing affordability and community social interaction.

› CONSIDERATIONS

›› Prospective residents who would benefit from, and contribute to, the vitality of agrihood developments may experience housing cost barriers if housing affordability is not addressed.

›› Developers may miss opportunities to promote community social interaction if they do not give special consideration to features that encourage engagement with food-production spaces.

› OPPORTUNITIES AND BEST PRACTICES

›› Develop a variety of housing types clustered in one area to promote community social interaction, including the following:

- ■ Single-family homes;
- ■ Duplexes;
- ■ Three- to four-story multifamily buildings; and
- ■ Homes for farmers and other employees.

›› Provide subsidized affordable and workforce housing and mixed-income/mixed-generational housing.

›› Consider innovative housing design solutions to promote affordability, such as modular homes, tiny homes, and cohousing.

›› Include project components to encourage engagement with food-production spaces, such as trails, edible landscaping, community gardens, shared kitchens, teaching gardens, and workshop/public gathering space.

MARIEL BEAUDOIN

Residents at Aria Denver have access to organic produce that is grown on site.

Serenbe is a 1,000-acre (405 ha) community in Chattahoochee Hills, Georgia, centered on a 25-acre (10 ha) professionally managed organic farm.

Greenhouse

People

Understand the range of necessary skills for community farmers, and make decisions about hiring and management accordingly.

❯ CONSIDERATIONS

» Project leaders face difficulties in identifying and recruiting farmers with the diverse skill sets necessary for project success.

» Investing in farmers and understanding their integral role in project success are essential, but plans should also be put in place for farm operations to continue should changes in farm leadership occur.

❯ OPPORTUNITIES AND BEST PRACTICES

» Develop a farm program at a project's outset that can advance regardless of employee turnover; document standard operating procedures to help with transitions and training new staff.

» Create clear job descriptions and set realistic expectations for farmers related to project goals, vision, and balance of time devoted to food production versus community events.

» Identify potential farmers and other employees through engagement with local universities and farmer workforce development organizations and by hosting on-site professional development and internship programs.

» At a minimum, pay farmers and workers who are employees a living wage and provide benefits.

» Explore profit-sharing models and other financial incentives to retain farmers; consider leasing land to self-employed farmers.

» Work to diversify the hiring pool by posting job descriptions in multiple languages and understanding cultural considerations.

Necessary Skills for Farmers at Agrihoods

- Patience and understanding

- Community engagement and communication skills

- Program management

- Strong work ethic demonstrated through past farming experiences

- Ability to coordinate, run, and manage public-facing events

- Planning and task management

- Multifaceted food-production experience

  - Business acumen and startup attitude

  - Finance, budgeting, and mathematical abilities

  - A passion for farming

  - Willingness to learn

  - Willingness to teach

  - Ability to "code switch" and balance various objectives

  - Ability to work in isolation for extended periods

  - Ability to manage

- Managing other employees

- Managing volunteers at community events

- Hosting and speaking at public meetings

People

Invest in homes for farmers and other farm employees.

› CONSIDERATIONS

›› Agrihoods can provide access to land and employment for farmers, but farmers may not be able to live nearby unless developers address housing affordability.

›› Opportunities for direct resident–farmer interaction are limited when farmers live off site.

› OPPORTUNITIES AND BEST PRACTICES

›› Consider providing free or subsidized homes for farmers as an investment in both employee satisfaction and project success.

›› Set clear policies related to who is eligible for free or subsidized homes; determine whether living on site is required and if housing is part of overall compensation.

›› Understand the complex dynamics of proximity to the farm for farmers:

■ Farmers often want to be part of the community but may not want to be on call for residents 24/7.

■ Farmers need to be close to crops and farm animals to respond to weather events and the like.

■ Some farmers may prefer to live on site, but others may simply want to live close by.

Agrihoods can provide access to land and employment for farmers.

RANCHO MISSION VIEJO LLC

A Day in the Life of a Farmer

Morning

Cock-a-doodle-doo! The morning harvest calls and the farmer rises to the occasion. The sun is just starting to shed its light. The sparkling dew rises from a field of lush green crops that have been nurtured for months and are now ready for harvest. The attire for such a task—knives, scissors, harvest crates, and an apron—must be rugged and ready for water, soil, prickly fruits, and leaves.

A glance at the whiteboard in the shed offers many harvest options—arugula, cilantro, kale, cucumbers, carrots, beets, flowers, herbs—but it's the carrots that are the priority this morning. Forty bunches are destined for the community-supported agriculture (CSA) program, 30 for the farm stand, and 20 for the local food pantry.

A big volunteer group has shown up to help with the harvest, so the farmer sneaks away to prep some beds for planting. First the tractor is inspected, filled with gas, and greased. The farmer drives the tractor through the fields to spread compost onto beds recently cleared from their last crop, then returns to till the compost into the soil before it gets baked by the sun.

Afternoon

The farmer works with a few interns on plantings—the seeds, seeding plates, and seeder are all loaded into a cart, along with markers and labels. The crew heads for the fields to sow the next succession of veggies, herbs, and flowers and to have lunch. They all take a break in the shade on the farm's event green under a beautiful tree, eating a lunch of fresh-picked salad, farm pickles, and sandwiches.

After lunch, one of the coordinators grabs the farmer to share some challenges she has been having with a new apprentice and asks for a meeting the next day. The farmer will have to find some other time to work on budgets and performance reviews! The farmer then makes sure the farm stand setup is going well. It looks like the produce has all been washed, bunched, weighed, documented in the harvest log, and orga-nized in the cooler. It is all nicely labeled for the farm stand, CSA, food pantry, restaurant, and local elementary school.

The farmer takes a few minutes to help volunteers load up the mobile farm stand that is headed to a health clinic to provide free, fresh produce to food-insecure families. Then the farmer thanks the local gleaning organization for bringing out so many volunteers to help with the harvest: "We couldn't have done it without you today!" says the farmer. "Please take a few pints of the strawberry seconds and big zucchinis. Look forward to seeing you all next week!"

Evening

It is now the evening and a band is playing during an on-site event. People are buzzing around the farm stand and food trucks, shopping for veggies and dinner, while families relax on picnic blankets and kids chase each other through bean tunnels, feed the baby sheep, and make vegetable art with the farm educators.

The farmer notices dozens of local families all getting to know each other. This is what it's all about: growing community through agriculture.

As the evening winds down, the farmer toasts the team, tucks the chickens away for the night, and grabs an armful of fresh eggs, veggies, and a flower bouquet to walk home. The farmer can't wait to hug the children, read them some books, and pass out from a full day of hard work, fun, and playing an integral role in the community.

Every Day

A day in the life of a farmer is guided by intuition, experience, observation, perseverance, and patience. It has many dynamic moving parts, such as the following:

- Operating equipment and tools safely and efficiently;

- Managing people responsibly and respectfully;

- Cultivating the land with sensitivity and respect;

- Engaging with and teaching visitors, volunteers, and students;

- Managing budgets and administrative aspects of running a business/nonprofit; and

- Caring for oneself and others to stay hydrated and injury free.

Partnerships

Collaborate with partners that share a common vision for agrihood development.

❯ CONSIDERATIONS

» The complexity of agrihood development and operations generally requires collaboration with organizations outside the "usual suspects" for developers.

» Developers may be challenged to identify appropriate project partners, given a lack of in-house knowledge of farming and farm-related programming needs.

» Creative partnerships require investment of time, resources, clear communication, and an entrepreneurial and collaborative spirit.

❯ OPPORTUNITIES AND BEST PRACTICES

» Attract key partners by sharing a clear project vision and a set of core values.

» Ensure that the organizational priorities of potential partners are aligned with one another and the overall agrihood project vision.

» Partner with entities that have a positive reputation in the community.

» Create partnership agreements that set out clear roles, responsibilities, and metrics for success.

» Value and respect the contributions partners make to agrihood development and operations; give partners decision-making authority related to their specific roles.

» Meet regularly to keep honest communication lines open.

» Revisit agreements and update them based on changes in programs, staffing, capacity, budgets, etc.

Increasing interest in locally grown food is leading to opportunities for developers to create projects that meet consumer demand by incorporating small farms and community food-growing areas.

SARAH ROBERSON

Groups to Engage to Ensure Project Success

- Municipalities and governing agencies
- Food, conservation, and community nonprofit organizations
- Farmers, farm consultants, and local farming associations
- Legal advisers
- Farm and agricultural master planners
- Lifestyle managers

- Higher education departments, educational organizations, and schools
- Faith-based institutions
- Philanthropic foundations
- Special interest groups
- County extension services
- Community thought leaders
- Corporate partners

Agrihoods are uniquely positioned to address health, sustainability, and social equity challenges.

RANCHO MISSION VIEJO LLC

Partnerships

Form partnerships to address health, sustainability, and social equity challenges through agrihood development and operations.

› CONSIDERATIONS

» Agrihoods are uniquely positioned to address health, sustainability, and social equity challenges, but project leaders must invest time to identify and cultivate appropriate partnerships to advance these goals.

» For agrihood operational models to be sustainable in the long term, project leaders may want to consider contributing to efforts to train the next generation of farmers.

› OPPORTUNITIES AND BEST PRACTICES

» Work with partners to create health-based educational and training programs that add value to the experience of residents and surrounding communities.

» Consider partnering with nonprofit organizations, higher education organizations, and medical associations to host classes that teach cooking, nutrition, and meal planning skills; find partners who can offer these programs in languages other than English spoken in the area.

» Explore opportunities to invest in community economic development by hosting job training programs focused on developing new farmers and skills for burgeoning food-based entrepreneurs.

» Use farms as a stage to educate youth about food growing and seasonality.

KEY INSIGHT: PARTNERSHIPS TO SUPPORT HEALTH

"Formal and informal partnerships can help developers, property owners, and managers build bridges, increase impact, and ensure the ongoing success of a project. Nontraditional partners include foundations, schools, health care providers, and health-focused nonprofits."

—ULI Building Healthy Places Toolkit

The 2018 ULI Growing the Field retreat at Coastal Roots Farm in Encinitas, California, brought together experts and practitioners working at the intersection of food and real estate to discuss best practices for agrihood development.

MYLES STEPHENS

Growing the Field retreat participants shared stories, approaches, successes, challenges, and lessons learned for the planning, development, and operation of agrihoods.

RACHEL MacCLEERY

CHAPTER 3

FURTHER CONSIDERATIONS

PUBLIC SECTOR GUIDELINES

Create land use and zoning policies to encourage the development of agrihoods.

› CONSIDERATIONS

» Zoning policies are often not set up to encourage or often even *allow* the development of farm-centered communities.

» Most zoning standards separate or limit allowable uses and specify minimum lots for housing, thereby making clustering of development difficult.

» Stakeholders—including public sector officials—lack understanding of the benefits of having a farm in the community.

» Many suburban and exurban communities face significant development pressures, potentially resulting in loss of farmland and open space.

» Local governments may be challenged to maintain infrastructure (roads, sewers, etc.) when development follows "traditional" suburban models.

» Zoning may not allow on-site events, weddings, and the like.

› OPPORTUNITIES AND BEST PRACTICES

» Include farming and food access considerations in zoning codes and general plans.

» Allow mixed-use development and uses complementary to working farms (event spaces, wine tasting rooms, parking, etc.).

» Consider incentivizing farming—for example, by offering reduced property tax assessments on agricultural land.

» Implement programs that allow communities to hold easements to permanently protect farmland, and direct development to areas with existing infrastructure.

» Consider deed restrictions, deeding the land to a third party, and/or development agreements to govern the development of a property.

Protected Agriculture/Limited Development Zoning, Kane County, Illinois

Kane County enacted a Protected Agriculture/Limited Development zoning designation in 2001 to both protect farmland and encourage farm-oriented communities in an area facing significant development pressures, just 40 miles west of Chicago. The zoning designation promotes a form of conservation design that provides for clustering of residential lots on a portion of the property and permanently protecting the remainder of the land for agriculture and open space.

Serosun Farms includes 300 acres (121 ha) of preserved farmland and restored upland and wetland prairie, savanna woodlands with walking trails, and stocked fishing ponds.

"Encouraging development, supporting agri-business, and conserving farmland go hand-in-hand. Clustering development around farms creates places that people want to live, while supporting local farmers and a community's rural character."

—JANICE HILL, EXECUTIVE PLANNER, KANE COUNTY, ILLINOIS

FREQUENTLY ASKED QUESTIONS

Q: What is the size range for agrihood food-production areas?

A: Agrihood food-production areas vary widely in size, depending on project goals and geography. Farms from less than one acre (0.4 ha) to more than 300 acres (120 ha) are common; orchards and ranchlands can be even larger—up to 20,000 acres (8,100 ha) or more. As a rule,

>> Farms less than five acres (2 ha) are typically more focused on education, experiences, and events with small-scale intensive production and require one to two full-time staff members;

>> Farms between five and 20 acres (2 to 8.1 ha) run much like a four- to five-acre (1.6 to 2 ha) farm, with more room for production and programming space, and require ten to 20 full-time staff members; and

>> Farms larger than 20 acres (8.1 ha) require more mechanization but can operate with fewer staff members because of greater efficiency from use of machinery.

Q: What types of foods are produced?

A: The types of foods produced differ depending on farm size, location, capacity, and project goals. Agrihoods produce everything from fruits and vegetables to eggs and meat. Some agrihoods even include olive groves, ranchlands for cattle grazing, and facilities for creating value-added products, such as wines, jams, and other prepared foods.

Q: Who does the farming?

A: Often, full-time farmers who are employees of the development company or homeowners association manage food production. Other models include resident food production and local farmers or nonprofit organizations leasing land from the developer or community land trust.

SEROSUN FARMS

Q: Do agrihoods include animals?

A: Some (but not all) agrihoods include animals, such as bees or poultry. Larger agrihoods with ranchlands may include livestock.

Q: Do agrihoods need barns or equipment sheds? How are crops watered?

A: Yes, structures such as barns and equipment sheds are important to support farm operations and provide space for programming. Approaches to irrigation vary based on geographical location. Drip irrigation is generally used on most crops; overhead irrigation is used in some locations, including pastures, event lawns, grassy paths, and cover crops.

Q: What is the typical cost per acre to operate a farm?

A: The cost per acre to operate a farm varies widely depending on location, crops grown, water, labor, programming, and many other factors. The first few acres are the most expensive because of the need to provide core infrastructure and public spaces. Other startup costs include hiring staff for base programming, administration, and food production.

Q: What are the tax benefits for farms and conserved farmland?

A: Most jurisdictions offer favorable property tax rates for agricultural land, depending on farm size and income—lower property tax rates can reduce the tax liability of investors. Farmland in conservation trusts/easements can qualify for local property tax savings or charitable tax deductions (if land is donated).[24]

Q: How do project leaders assure residents or homebuyers that farmland is not going to be developed in the future?

A: Methods for long-term farmland conservation include conservation easements, deed restrictions, development agreements, and deeding the land to a third party.

Q: How does the farm generate income? Will it have to be subsidized?

A: Farms will generally require subsidies at a project's outset but can become break-even or profitable within a few years, depending on factors such as size, food-production capacity, and ability to host revenue-generating events.

Farm operational costs can be offset by food sales, but farms may need to rely on support from the development—especially during early project phases—in the form of free or subsidized land, contributions from transfer fees, homeowners association fees, and other mechanisms.

GROWING THE FIELD

Each day, developers, investors, designers, and other real estate and land use professionals make decisions about their projects and set priorities based on current and anticipated market trends, community needs, and financial constraints.[25]

Each new project presents opportunities for developers and other project stakeholders to invest in a community's health, well-being, social cohesion, environmental sustainability, and overall quality of life.

Including food-production spaces in development projects can help ensure project success and achieve social and environmental goals. Agrihoods, individually and as a whole, have terrific potential to help address challenges in our existing food system and development models. For this potential to be realized, a new "field" of agrihood developers and practitioners must be created.

The Bridgespan Group, a U.S. nonprofit organization that provides management consulting to nonprofits and philanthropists, defines a "field" as a community of organizations and individuals working together toward a common goal and using a set of common approaches to achieve that goal.[26]

A new field for agrihoods—comprising developers, designers, financial leaders, farmers and operators, and others—will be necessary for this development type to become common practice across the development landscape.

THE STRONG FIELD FRAMEWORK

Shared-identity community aligned around a common purpose and a set of core values

Standards of practice	Knowledge base	Leadership and grassroots support	Funding and supporting policy
• Codification of standards of standards of practice • Exemplary models and resources (e.g., how-to guides) • Available resources to support implementation (e.g., technical assistance) • Respected credentialing/ ongoing professional development training for practitioners and leaders	• Credible evidence that practice achieves desired outcomes • Community of researchers to study and advance practice • Vehicles to collect, analyze, debate and disseminate knowledge	• Influential leaders and exemplary organizations across key segments of the field (e.g., practitioners, researchers, business leaders, policy makers) • Broad base of support from major constituencies	• Enabling policy environment that supports and encourages model practices • Organized funding streams from public, philanthropic, and corporate sources of support

Adapted from: *Bridgespan Group*, The Strong Field Framework: A Guide and Toolkit for Funders and Nonprofits Committed to Large-Scale Impact *(Boston: James Irvine Foundation, 2009), www.bridgespan.org/insights/library/philanthropy/the-strong-field-framework-a-guide-and-toolkit-for.*

What does the Bridgespan field framework mean for agrihoods? Overall, it means that a lot of work still remains to be done, and that a lot of opportunity exists for the practice to evolve, mature, and become recognized as a viable and successful development model.

For agrihood development to become a field, the following elements will be necessary:

» **Shared identity:** A shared narrative, brand, and goals for the agrihood movement and for agrihood projects;

» **Standards of practice:** Best practices that improve the quality and success of individual projects and ensure the integrity and growth of the field as a whole;

» **Knowledge base:** Knowledge shared across practitioners to improve the success of projects and grow the talent pipeline, including training, tours, and potential accreditation programs;

» **Leadership and grassroots support:** Support from multiple sectors and influential leaders; and

» **Funding and supporting policy:** Resources and policies that support its growth.

ULI and its partners are eager to help support and facilitate the thoughtful evolution of the field of agrihood development, so that the great potential and opportunity of agrihoods—for people, communities, and the planet—can be realized.

Potential Long-Term Success Measures for the "Agrihood Movement"

Participants at ULI's 2018 Growing the Field retreat developed the following list of potential long-term success measures for the "agrihood movement":

■ Widespread recognition that food production and "working lands" should be standard development components;

■ A shared narrative and shared values that help define the field;

■ Shared resources and platform for sharing these resources (or channels to distribute shared resources and engage in regular communications);

■ A defined structure for the field;

■ High demand for participation at future agrihood-focused events and retreats;

■ Collection and dissemination of additional quantitative data on agrihood home sales;

■ Learning about agrihoods via word of mouth;

■ A system for prospective agrihood developers to learn from and/or tour established projects;

■ Growth in the number of farmers interested in working at agrihoods and in farmer job opportunities and training programs;

■ Increased public interest in local food and farming;

■ Local jurisdictions approaching developers to ask for agrihood development; and

■ Programs providing training and accreditation for aspiring agrihood community farmers.

1. Urban Land Institute, *America in 2015: A ULI Survey of Views on Housing, Transportation, and Community* (Washington, DC: Urban Land Institute, 2015), http://uli.org/wp-content/uploads/ULI-Documents/America-in-2015.pdf.

2. Harvard Women's Health Watch, "The Benefits of Strong Relationships," December 2010, https://www.health.harvard.edu/newsletter_article/the-health-benefits-of-strong-relationships.

3. Dennis Jerke, Douglas R. Porter, and Terry J. Lassar, *Urban Design and the Bottom Line* (Washington, DC: Urban Land Institute, 2008).

4. Centers for Disease Control and Prevention, "Adult Obesity Facts," last updated August 13, 2018, https://www.cdc.gov/obesity/data/adult.html.

5. Urban Land Institute, *America in 2015: A ULI Survey of Views on Housing, Transportation, and Community* (Washington, DC: Urban Land Institute, 2015), http://uli.org/wp-content/uploads/ULI-Documents/America-in-2015.pdf.

6. American Farmland Trust, "Farmers," https://www.farmland.org/our-work/areas-of-focus/farmers.

7. Funders' Network for Smart Growth and Livable Communities, "Investing in Healthy, Sustainable Places through Urban Agriculture," Translation Paper 5, ed. 2, 2011, https://www.fundersnetwork.org/files/learn/Investing_in_Urban_Agriculture_Final_110713.pdf.

8. Colorado Health Foundation, *Food Access in Colorado* (Denver, CO: Colorado Health Foundation, 2010), https://www.coloradohealth.org/sites/default/files/documents/2017-01/TCHF_Food_Access_Report_web-Food%20Access%20in%20CO.pdf.

9. Sasha Feldstein and James Barham, *Running a Food Hub: Learning from Food Hub Closures,* Service Report 77, vol. 4 (Washington, DC: U.S. Department of Agriculture, 2017), https://www.rd.usda.gov/files/publications/SR77_FoodHubs_Vol4_0.pdf.

10. American Farmland Trust, "No Farms No Food," https://www.farmland.org/no-farms-no-food.

11. Sarah Dewerdt, "Is Local Food Better?," Worldwatch Institute website, http://www.worldwatch.org/node/6064

12 John M. Mandyck and Eric B. Schultz, *Food Foolish* (Carrier Corporation, 2015), http://foodfoolishbook.naturalleader.com/.

13. Christopher L. Webber and H. Scott Matthews, "Food-Miles and the Relative Climate Impacts of Food Choices in the United States," *Environmental Science and Technology* 42, no. 10 (2008): 3508–3513, https://pubs.acs.org/doi/10.1021/es702969f.

14. Webber and Matthews, "Food-Miles."

15. U.S. Environmental Protection Agency, "Smart Growth," What are some environmental benefits of smart growth strategies?, last updated May 1, 2018, https://www.epa.gov/smartgrowth/about-smart-growth#benefits.

16. Urban Land Institute, *Cultivating Development: Trends and Opportunities at the Intersection of Food and Real Estate* (Washington, DC: Urban Land Institute, 2016), https://uli.org/wp-content/uploads/ULI-Documents/Cultivating-Development-Trends-and-Opportunities-at-the-Intersection-of-Food-and-Real-Estate.pdf.

17. A. Cort Sinnes, "Food Gardening in the U.S. at the Highest Levels in More Than a Decade According to New Report by the National Gardening Association," *National Gardening Association Learning Library*, April 2, 2014, https://garden.org/learn/articles/view/3819/.

18. Organic Trade Association, "Robust Organic Sector Stays on Upward Climb, Posts New Records in U.S. Sales," PR Newswire, May 24, 2017, https://www.prnewswire.com/news-releases/robust-organic-sector-stays-on-upward-climb-posts-new-records-in-us-sales-300463127.html.

19. National Count of Farmers Market Directory Listings, USDA-AMS-Marketing Services Division, https://www.ams.usda.gov/sites/default/files/media/NationalCountofFMDirectory17.JPG.

20. Dennis Jerke, Douglas R. Porter, and Terry J. Lassar, *Urban Design and the Bottom Line* (Washington, DC: Urban Land Institute, 2008).

21. Cluster/Open Space Development, Chester County Planning Commission, http://www.chescoplanning.org/MuniCorner/Tools/Cluster.cfm.

22. Organic Trade Association, "Robust Organic Sector Stays on Upward Climb, Posts New Records in U.S. Sales," PR Newswire, May 24, 2017, https://www.prnewswire.com/news-releases/robust-organic-sector-stays-on-upward-climb-posts-new-records-in-us-sales-300463127.html.

23. Urban Land Institute, *Cultivating Development: Trends and Opportunities at the Intersection of Food and Real Estate* (Washington, DC: Urban Land Institute, 2016), https://americas.uli.org/report/cultivating-development-trends-opportunities-intersection-food-real-estate/.

24. "The Tax Advantages of Investing in Agriculture," *Harvest Returns* blog, May 23, 2017, https://www.harvestreturns.com/blog/2017/5/23/the-tax-advantages-of-investing-in-agriculture.

25. Urban Land Institute, *Building Healthy Places Toolkit: Strategies for Enhancing Health in the Built Environment* (Washington, DC: Urban Land Institute, 2015), http://uli.org/wp-content/uploads/ULI-Documents/Building-Healthy-Places-Toolkit.pdf.

26. Bridgespan Group, *The Strong Field Framework: A Guide and Toolkit for Funders and Nonprofits Committed to Large-Scale Impact* (Boston: James Irvine Foundation, 2009), https://www.bridgespan.org/insights/library/philanthropy/the-strong-field-framework-a-guide-and-toolkit-for.

ACKNOWLEDGMENTS

The Urban Land Institute gratefully acknowledges the contributions of the following people to this report.

Participants in the ULI Growing the Field retreat at Coastal Roots Farm/Leichtag Commons, March 21–23, 2018

Daniel Allen
Farmscape

Thomas Blessent
HomeFed Corporation

JD Cerince Brown
Farm to Fork

Sona Desai
Coastal Roots Farm

Debra DeWald
Serosun Farms

John T. DeWald
JDA

Wendy DeWitt
San Diego Housing Commission

Jim Farley
Leichtag Foundation

Ann Cutner Firestone
Solutions for Urban Agriculture

Heather Foley
ULI San Diego–Tijuana

Clayton Garrett
Edible Group LLC

Amaya Genaro
Rancho Mission Viejo

Ninia Hammond
Integral Communities

Monica Hollins
Freehold Communities

Daron "Farmer D" Joffe
Farmer D Consulting

Patience Kabwasa
Colorado Springs Food Rescue

Mary Kimball
Center for Land-Based Learning

Warren King
Food Commons Fresno Community Corporation

Sandra Kulli
Kulli Marketing

Shane Lory
Colorado Springs Food Rescue

Christian Macke
122 West Landscape Architecture

Amie MacPhee
Cultivate

Adam McCurdy
Coastal Roots Farm

James A. Moore
Jacobs

Cory Mosser
Natural Born Tillers

Ari Novy
Leichtag Foundation

Steve Nygren
Serenbe

Greg Ramsey
Village Habitat Design

Halé Richardson
HomeFed Corporation

Sarah Rosenberger
Farm to Fork

Dwight Saathoff
Project Finance & Development

Charlene Seidle
Leichtag Foundation

Sri Sethuratnam
Center for Land-Based
Learning

Teri Slavik-Tsuyuki
tst ink LLC

Scott Snodgrass
Agmenity

Michael J. Sweeney
Land Concern

Jennifer York
Leichtag Foundation

· · · · · · · · · · · · · · · · · · · ·
Additional interviewees, advisers,
and resources
· · · · · · · · · · · · · · · · · · · ·

Rick Bagel
Wetrock Farm

Mariel Beaudoin
Urban Ventures LLC

Les Bluestone
Blue Sea Development

Wendy Hawthorne
Groundwork Denver

Janice Hill
Kane County, Illinois

Dave Hutchinson
Kukui'ula

Alann Krivor
Skokomish Farms

Mali Krivor
Skokomish Farms

Brad Leibov
Liberty Prairie Foundation

Travis Marcotte
The Intervale

Monica Olsen
Serenbe

Susan Powers
Urban Ventures LLC

Matthew "Quint" Redmond
Agriburbia

Steffen Schneider
Hawthorne Valley Farm

Thomas Woliver
Hillwood Communities